# My Prayer

*Lord, open my eyes mind, that I may so acknowledge that You are the one, true God and besides You, there is no other. In the almighty name of Christ Jesus, amen.*

If you're in the bondage of drug addiction, may I humbly recommend these two resources:

miraclehill.org

wisdominlivinglife.org

# Table of Contents

Forward ~ Come to Me ............................................................ page 5

First of All ............................................................................... page 6

Drugs ~ The Great Deceiver ................................................... page 9

My Testimony ......................................................................... page 12

So You're Off Drugs... Now What? ....................................... page 18

Trusting God .......................................................................... page 20

Literally Looking for Love in All the Wrong Places ............ page 22

Building Relationships ........................................................... page 24

Letting the Past Sleep ............................................................ page 25

Trials, Tears of Joy, Tears of Pain ......................................... page 26

Growing in My Knowledge of God ........................................ page 33

A Poem for the Ladies ............................................................ page 42

Philippians 4:8 ........................................................................ page 43

An Invitation ........................................................................... page 45

# Forward

*"Come to Me, all you who labor and are heavy laden, and I will give you rest."* Matthew 11:28 ESV

This book is for the glory of God through Jesus and the sweet communion of the Holy Spirit. It is my prayer that the Lord will use this book to free many from the bondage of addiction. My addiction just happened to be drugs. It's been said that the insanity of addiction of any sort is doing the same thing over and over, expecting different results.

I believe addiction is a form of idolatry. When we receive what we desire, we experience a false sense of satisfaction at first that sucks us into a deceptive need and before long, whether acknowledged or not, it becomes a sick form of worship… it becomes our god… something we cannot live without.

Only when we worship the one true God, Jesus Christ, will we find real satisfaction and complete freedom from addiction.

"No pit is so deep, that He is not deeper still." Corrie Ten Boom

# Thank You!

*First of all, I give glory, honor, and praise to God, to my Lord and Savior, Jesus Christ, through whom all blessings flow and to the Holy Spirit, the giver of good gifts.*

I would also like to thank:

Ross and Janiece Robinson, for encouraging me to "keep writing my heart to God."

Matt and Katie Nestberg and Allan Sherer, for encouraging me to share my gift with the Church body.

Pastor Peter Hubbard, who always prayed with me.

Joel and Peggy Taylor, who took me into their home with their kids and loved on me and prayed for me daily.

Dale and Barbi Haase and family, who had us Renewal ladies in their home once a month for mouth-watering meals and fellowship.

Kim Hull, who God used mightily in my time at Renewal, as well as Josh and Gini Hewitt.

Keith Garrett, who always spoke God's truth into my life without fear or question.

Dear Mary Carolyn Garton, who encouraged me to be salt and light to everyone I meet.

Alan Bunn, a great encouragement to me through his teaching Life Ed classes when I was in Renewal.

Jim and Ginger Evans, for their friendship.

The staff of Miracle Hill Shepherd's Gate, especially my friend Carrie Seills, for all the prayers, discipline and encouragement and Janine Slocum who gave me grace on many occasions!

To my prayer warrior sisters: Phyllis Swartz, Susan Raines, Deb Stoeber, Susan Wood, Lynn Adams, Rebecca Davis, and my BFF, Angela Gambrell.

To Winn and Rhonda Freeman of Wisdom in Living Life Ministries, the HaPiSo shepherding group, and the staff of North Hills Community Church, for their fellowship and love.

To the love of my life, my mother, Lola Mae Irby, who never stopped praying for or loving me.

# Drugs, the Great Deceiver

There have been times, many times, that I would stop using drugs, and was under the delusion that I was okay when in fact I had grieved the Holy Spirit into silence, and that is a dangerous place to be. It is in fact, an open door for the enemy of our soul. I noticed that every time I would relapse, this passage of Scripture came to mind:

*"When the unclean spirit has gone out of a person, it passes through waterless places seeking rest, and finding none it says, 'I will return to my house from which I came.' And when it comes, it finds the house swept and put in order. Then it goes and brings seven other spirits more evil than itself, and they enter and dwell there. And the last state of that person is worse than the first." (Luke: 24-26 ESV).*

That is the deception and delusion of believing that you can go out and get high 'just one more time' and feel guilty or convicted (depending on the state of your heart) moreso every time you go back out and use. Dear believer, don't believe the lie that when you become a Christian, you can still do as you please and go to church on Sunday and play church. I did it for years and would go out and live under the delusion that I was living life on my own terms.

*"Do not be deceived, God is not mocked, for whatever one sows, that he will also reap." (Galatians 6:7 ESV)*

"And do not be drunk with wine…"
Ephesians 5:18

## Drugs, the Great Deceiver

It's okay to drink a little wine

You'll feel a little giddy
    And all is fine

Then all of a sudden
    It's not enough

Just a little marijuana when I awake
    And feeling kinda rough

"Let me introduce myself
    My name is cocaine

When wine and marijuana don't cut it
    Just call my name

I'll take you to another planet and then
    When you get back,
    You'll want to go back again."

"But hey!
    Don't worry.
        I've got your back.
            I'm cocaine's offspring;
                Just call me crack!

I'll take you where none of the others
    Have taken you before.

And when you come back,
    You'll want some more.

And when you go and pawn
    That ring on your finger,
    Then

        BAM!

I've got you hook, line, and sinker."

So whether it be liquid, solid, powder, or pills
    It's all drugs, and it all kills

And when you get in that pit of despair
    And lose your will

Remember that God is
    Deeper still

So give it all to Jesus
    And give up the dope

And allow the power of the Holy Spirit to fill you with hope.

# My Testimony

I am the youngest of seven children. My siblings are much older than I, so I played by myself quite a bit. We were a normal family, from an American standpoint.

My father died from a massive heart attack at the young age of 45. I was devastated... my father was my whole world. My mother worked very hard to provide for us and did without many things for herself to make sure that we were provided for.

When I entered high school, I began to experiment with wine and before long, I was a full-blown drunk. I began to smoke marijuana in the mornings so that I would be able to function throughout the day. I became pregnant in my junior year of high school and I was pretty much an absentee mom. A year later, I became pregnant with my second child and allowed him to be adopted when he was an infant. By this time, I was running up and down the Eastern Seaboard trying to "find myself" and eventually met a man whom I thought was "the man of my dreams."

That dream became a nightmare. I was forced into prostitution and the verbal abuse became physical. I ran away several times, but he would always "sweet talk" me into going back with him to Florida. You may think that I'm stupid for going back to him, but if you've ever been in an abusive relationship, it is literally domestic terrorism.

One day after 14 years of abuse, I came to the revelation that if I didn't leave this man, one of us was going to die and it wasn't going to be me! I failed to mention that I became pregnant by this man and he tried to get me to have an abortion and I refused by basically hiding the pregnancy until it was obvious. After I gave birth to a third child, I walked out of the hospital and left her there because drugs were more important. She was adopted by a sweet Christian couple and when she became an adult she forgave me without question and never brought the subject up again.

I continued to abuse drugs and had a one-night stand with the same man who had abused me all those years and became pregnant with my fourth child. This child was taken from me as soon as she was born because I had abused my body and hers with drugs and I was sent to prison.

After being release, I continued to use drugs. One night I had a strange dream involving balloons blowing up and exploding When I woke up my legs were so swollen that the rubber in my socks had literally come apart. I was rushed to the ER and the eight Doctors around my hospital bed were baffled as to why my entire body was so swollen. Many tests later I was given a biopsy where they found 5 hidden Fibroid Tumors, each the size of a human head. I remained hospitalized for 13 days and was released.

Upon leaving the hospital I returned to the hotel room I was sharing with a man. I immediately began to smoke crack-cocaine.

Three months later, I began having severe stomach cramps. The pain increased until I was screaming and yelling at the hotel clerk to call 911. I was taken to the hospital where seven days later I awoke. The doctors informed me that my small intestine was severely inflamed and they had to keep me heavily medicated to relieve the inflammation before performing surgery. I had a great part of my small intestine removed and was hospitalized for 9 days.

I was released from the hospital but my body was not sewn up. It was left open, covered with dressings in order for it to heal from the inside out. A nurse would come to my hotel room daily to change the dressings until I was able to do it on my own. I still continued to abuse drugs with my body opened and it is only by the grace of God that I'm not dead. I was on a downward spiral, on my way to hell with a bullet!

After 33 years of this hellish lifestyle and a subsequent rape by someone I thought was a friend, I asked my niece to call the police. I was taken to the hospital where I had a mental breakdown and was transferred to a mental facility where I remained for 30 days.

However, after being released I went back to the lifestyle that I was accustomed to. I started abusing alcohol again (which, by the way, is a drug) with crack-cocaine and ended up losing my job. I was then hired at a 5-star hotel as a Banquet Bar-Tender and did Room Service as well. Pleased with my work performance, I was given extra hours and began to snort cocaine and drink Red Bulls in order to stay "energized and alert." I ended up back in the hospital for a week with Peptic Ulcers in my stomach. My attitude became so awful that it cost me my job yet again.

I got on my knees that night and cried out to God to take the alcohol from me and in the year 2000, He did... but I surrendered with one hand behind my back, because I wasn't ready to let go of the cocaine.

I ended up smoking crack-cocaine again and it was so much worse, it wasn't fun anymore. I ended up homeless and alone, I went to the ER and told the nurse that I needed help with my drug addiction and I was sent to a detoxification center and from there to a place in Greenville, S.C. called Miracle Hill Shepherd's Gate Women and Children's Shelter. There I remained and obtained employment at The Waffle House.

My birthday came up and I decided to go out after work and celebrate and so I relapsed. Matthew 12:43-45a says: "When the unclean spirit has gone out of a person, it passes through waterless places seeking rest, but finds none. Then it says, I will go back to my house from which I came. And when it comes, it finds the house empty, swept, and put in order. Then it goes and finds seven other spirits more evil than itself, and they enter in and dwell there, and the last state of that person is worse than the first." And so it is when you relapse.

We were given random drug tests at Shepards Gate, so we had just been given drug tests 2 days earlier, but I was so convicted by The Holy Spirit, that I went and confessed to staff that I'd been using. I was asked to leave the next day. So I checked into a Hotel and continued to abuse drugs; it was the worse two weeks of my life, no one wanted to be around me, including the people I did drugs with ( God was at work). Finally, I called my oldest daughter and she came and picked me up, drove me to my mom's house where I was called everything but a child of God, I couldn't blame them, I'd put my family through so much. My niece was in the Hospital, waiting to go and be with The Lord and she begged me to go and seek help for my drug addiction. I went to the nearest phone and called Miracle Hill Shepards Gate, which also had a Christ-centered drug rehab called Renewal. By the grace of God, I got in the next day, and my niece went to be with The Lord 3 days later. After 6 months, I graduated from Renewal in November of 2005. I have a number of health issues, many as a result of drug abuse, but I am no longer addicted and I serve an awesome God who will never forsake me, I am not a recovering addict, and my identity is Mrs. Jesus Christ!

My life verse is Romans 8:38-39:

*For I am convinced that neither death, nor life, nor angels, nor principalities, nor things present, nor things to come, nor powers, nor height, nor depth, nor anything in all creation will be able to separate (Lynn) from the love of God, which is in Christ Jesus, our Lord.*

"And do not be conformed to the pattern of this world..." Romans 12:2

## No Longer a Recovering Addict

I'm no longer a recovering addict
    I have been set apart
Ever since I asked my Lord and Savior, Jesus
    To come into my heart

No longer do I read the secular self-help books
    Sold in stores all across the nation
I'm no longer a recovering addict
    I'm in the process of sanctification!

No longer do I believe the lie
    The lie of low self-esteem
I'm no longer a recovering addict
    For by the blood of my Lord and Savior, Jesus
    The Christ
    I am redeemed!

Christ died for all mankind
    No exceptions or exemptions
By God's grace, I'm not here to celebrate recovery
    I'm here to celebrate Redemption!

# So You're Off the Drugs... Now What?

After graduating from Miracle Hill's Renewal Center, a Christ-centered drug rehabilitation facility for women, I remained in Greenville, South Carolina and became a member of North Hills Community Church. I got involved in a Shepherding Group and began pursuing a deeper relationship with God. I prayerfully sought out a mentor and began attending ladies Bible study and formed life-long friendships with some very godly women. I praised God that I didn't have to walk around being spiritual, but just be Lynn (the new creature in Christ).

All things new, bright, and beautiful, I testified at church every time the opportunity arose... then the world was thrust at me like a bullet! Praise God for His Spirit living on the inside empowering me, convicting me when I'm wrong (every day) and convincing me to do right (all the time). There were times, lots of times, when I would question God's will for my life and He's was always faithful to give me blessed assurance. I admit that I was quite fearful when trials began to come into my life as I have come to call "valley fear" but God's word consistently reminded me that He is the Great High Priest Who has been tempted in all ways as we are, yet without sin (Hebrews 4:15).

I know in my heart that I've been bought with a price that I will never be able to pay. As long as He gives me the grace to do so, I will tell anyone who, by His grace, has gotten off drugs (by the way, alcohol is a drug, too!) that Jesus died for the addicted as well and the Holy Spirit will give you all the strength you need to combat "Valley Fear."

> "For you were bought with a price."
> 1 Corinthians 6:20a

## Valley Fear

After being "bought" out of the pit of drug addiction
    All was well I thought I'd have no more afflictions

Until the Holy Spirit spoke to me in such a way as to remind me
    That I must go through the valley some day.

Of course, I didn't want to leave my comfort zone
    But He gently reminded me Who's on The Throne

By telling me that Jesus went through the lowest of the low
    So who are you that you can't go?

I then remembered that when Jesus hung on that tree
    He saved a slimy piece of worm-ridden filth like me
    And Hallelujah! I will be with Him throughout eternity.

So when your time comes for the valley to go through
    Just remember, Jesus went ahead of you!

# Trusting God

There came a particular time in my life (though I would not admit it at the time) where I didn't trust God to come through for me; He wasn't moving fast enough (for me, it was all about ME!) and my finances were not equal to my lifestyle (I didn't follow my financial adviser's advice).

I began to cry out to God for help. My working hours got cut and I didn't tell my financial adviser. In fact, I lied to every one for two solid years, (trying to look spiritual, but instead, I was looking abominable in my pride suit) and yielded to the temptation of payday loans.

It worked for a time until I started borrowing from one to pay off the other, and I was so convicted and stressed out to where I literally became so physically ill, I thought that I would go into cardiac arrest! I stopped going to Shepherding group and isolated myself (big mistake!) from everyone. Well, my Father loved me enough to discipline me severely. I had to give up my apartment, my pride, and I confessed and asked forgiveness from every one I had lied to.

And my God is so faithful; even though I had to give up everything material, I've learned to cling to the only One who gave up everything for me on the Cross of Calvary. I trust and believe that God's timing is always perfect - you must trust God!

"The Lord is my Light and my Salvation, whom shall I fear?" Psalm 27:1a

# Psalm 27:1

You must trust God, you must trust God
When things don't go as planned or seem rather odd
You must trust Him every second of each day

Just trust Him, for He is the only Way to heaven, you see

Christ died and rose that we may be with Him in eternity

If you're in Christ, the Holy Spirit resides inside
The Lord is my light and my salvation
Why in the world shall I fear or hide

For I know the God that I serve
He is waiting for me at the end of the narrow road which
Leads straight to Jesus and there's not even a curve

If the road that you're on doesn't go straight up
Ask Christ into your life
And the Holy Spirit will fill your cup to
Overflowing so much so
That you could not possibly begin to understand

Just trust the One who holds your next breath
In His holy nail-scarred hands

# Literally Looking for Love in All the Wrong Places

As a younger woman, I was teased and taunted quite a bit and as a result, I had no self-esteem. I began to do whatever it takes to be "popular" by sleeping with whoever had shown me "affection." So it was, as a result of all this "affection," I gave birth to four children. These children would have given me love, but in my blind pursuit of love (if you will), their's "wasn't the 'love' I wanted... I couldn't be free to be me" (what a joke!).

So I began the downward spiral of drugs, prostitution, and unspeakable things, all in the twisted name of "love." I endured, only by the grace of my Savior (though I didn't see it at the time) 14 years of physical, sexual and the worst of all, verbal abuse. Physical wounds eventually heal, but verbal abuse penetrates the heart. Whoever wrote "sticks and stones will break my bones, but names (or words) will never hurt me," was ignorant to the fact that death and life are in the power of the tongue...
Proverbs 18:12a.

I am so very thankful for the unconditional Love of Jesus, the Lover of my soul, who loves me unconditionally!

"For God so loved the world..." John 3:16

# Real Love Forever

I was so sick in my sin
Until Jesus entered in
And now I know what real love is

I was looking for love in the wrong direction
It was superficial
There was no affection

And then I met the Lover of my soul
Who picked me up and made me whole!

And I'm gonna love Him for the rest of my life
In Him there's no stressing, no drama, no strife

The One who's loved me from eternity past
Is mine, all mine, and it will always last

I'm gonna love You, Jesus
For of the universe, You are the Eternal Light
For Your finished work on the Cross is real Love for eternal life!

# Building Relationships

*"We must give up the vain idea of trying to please everybody. It is impossible, and the attempt is a mere waste of time. We must be content to walk in Christ's steps and let the world say what it likes."*
J. C. Ryle

I don't want to give the impression that after becoming sober, life was blissful, because it was anything but! I'd put my family, to put it mildly, through quite a bit. I had to gain their trust, ask forgiveness for what I'd put them through, and show them, by the grace of God, walking with Him, that the change in me was, in fact, real. There were family members that it had taken five years to convince that my walk with The Lord was genuine, with no turning back. Going back to my old lifestyle was not an option; I was done, with the help of The Holy Spirit. Do I still have issues with certain family members? Absolutely! But I no longer feel as if I have to continually convince them that I'm not Lynn, the drunken drug addict. I've learned that no matter how hard you try, someone is not going to be happy and I didn't want to slip back into the trap of people pleasing, which is in fact, idolatry. I have a relationship with two of my four birth children, and Lord willing I pray that I will hear from the other two, someday.

# Letting the Past Sleep

It never ceases to amaze me how some "friends" that claim to be there for you, have a tendency to always slide your past into a conversation that has absolutely nothing to do with the subject matter. The conversation can be on how to bake cookies and all of a sudden, "friend" says, "Well at least you ain't cooking crack no more!" And I'm thinking: "There's a reason it's called the past, let it sleep!"

Or I can run into someone I used to attend church with and this individual will say (where everyone in America can hear it), "Well, at least you're not drinking that liquor, or smoking that crack, and leaving that child with your mother no more!" And I have to reply: "Maybe because she's 36 years old now?!"

Worst of all, when I first graduated from Miracle Hill Renewal Center, I thought that the Lord put me on earth to tell everybody I met my testimony (in it's entirety!) and a dear friend of mine reminded me and assured me that wasn't necessary! Now when encountered by an individual from my past I wait for an opening, not to share my testimony, but to share the Gospel of Jesus Christ. Not all are receptive at the moment, but the seed has been sown. Someone else may water, but it is God who gives the increase!

# Trials, Tears of Joy, Tears of Pain

I'm a crier by nature - have always had a tender heart. I cry at weddings, funerals, worship services, you name it, I cry at it! I should've been one of those paid mourners, like in the Old Testament at the funerals, they would hire people to wail and cry, I'd be quite wealthy.

In all seriousness, I cry a lot more frequently because of the pain in my entire body. The pain is constant and causes me to cry out to God for his blessed assurance in the midst of the suffering. Then I find I am able to rejoice and thank Him for the pain, because it's drawing me ever so nearer, deeper, into more intimate relationship with my Lord who will always be there and will never leave, nor forsake me (Hebrews 13:5b). Nothing can separate me from his love (Romans 8:39b).

I cry tears of joy because I'm no longer in bondage to sin (Romans 6:18), I have been set free. If the Son sets you free, you will be free indeed (John 8:36). On those days (and there are many) that I cannot get out of bed, I can cry... and cry out because I know my Savior sees my tears, and in this I rejoice!

# He Knows

I know my Savior sees my tears
    My hurts
    My pain
    And calms my fears

That He always has for me His best
    And someday will give me eternal rest from
    All the trials and evil of this world
Ever since I was just a girl
    I have always felt Him tugging at my heart
    Reminding me that
    Even from eternity past I am a part of
    His perfect holy master plan
    And that His returning is close at hand

Even though at times His returning seems far and away
    The Holy Spirit reminds me that with God
    A day is as a thousand years,
        And a thousand years
        As a day.

When Christ returns
    With joy and excitement the heavens and earth
        Shall quake and testify
    In one accord that
    He indeed was
    Well worth
    The wait!

# Living on My Own
# Living on a Budget

Living on my own was a challenge, mainly because I wasn't being honest with my financial advisor (I strongly advise you to find one in your church). I began to supplement my income by borrowing money from pay day loan stores.

I became addicted to seeing the money in my bank account, so I ended up borrowing money from several pay day loan stores, borrowing from Peter to pay Paul, if you will. Before long, actually two years later, lying to everyone about staying accountable, I owed hundreds of dollars to four different stores.

After being so stressed out from hiding my sin from everyone but God, I was so convicted that I became physically ill with chest pains and I literally thought that I was having a heart attack! I then confessed my sin to my financial advisor and my Sheparding Group and it was suggested that I move out of my apartment and into a sweet family's home whom I'd lived with before until I paid off all of my debts. It was a humbling experience, to say the least, and a lesson learned. This experience taught me that absolute dependence on God is the only way to go.

*"And my God will supply every need of yours according to His riches in glory in Christ Jesus."* Philippians 4:19 ESV

# Praise Him

*Praise Him when times are good*
*Praise Him when times are bad*
*Praise Him when you're happy*
*Praise Him when you're sad*

*Praise Him when you're ready to pout*
*Rant, rave, and pull your hair out!*

*Jesus knows just how you feel*
*Six hours one Friday He made it real*

*Whipped, beaten, spat upon*
*Atop His sweet, bloody Head was a crown of thorns*

*Humiliated, stripped naked*
    *Rusty nails in His Hands and Feet*
      *Never did such sweet love and sorrow meet*

*It should have been me*
*It should have been you*

*But as Jesus hung on that Cross*
    *Through sweet bloody swollen lips looked down and said,*
    *"I loved you with an everlasting love,"*
*When all was lost*
*So praise Him, without ceasing, for bearing your cross*

# Are You Rejoicing?

It's oh so easy to rejoice
    When the waters are calm
    The skies are blue
    No cause for alarm

But are you still rejoicing
    When the clouds roll in
    And the calm becomes a storm
    And raging wind?

Are you hearing the still small voice
    In the mist of the stormy sea
    Saying, "Sufficient for you, is the grace of Me?"

Then be at peace, dear believer
    Rejoice and sing;

For the Lord hides you
    In the shelter of His wings!

Rejoice in times of calm
    And in times of storms
    For underneath are the Everlasting Arms

"Sufficient for you is the grace of Me"-2Cor. 12:9

# The Peace of God

For a deeper relationship with God, I prayed
I want to be more intimate with You
Never even beginning to conceive of
The depths of which He was about to take me through

My trial, which included much physical suffering
Which God allowed, this is true
But in the midst of my pain and suffering, He said,
"Don't be discouraged my child, I've got you."

The peace of God washed over me
    as of the releasing of a pent-up flood
        But Hallelujah!
It is what it is, when you've been taken deep into God's love

My joy is unspeakable, unimaginable
Never have I experienced such a wonderful thing before
It is the peace of God that surpasses all understanding
When you put your faith in the One who is tha Door

I cannot say I liked this pain with my life being all amiss
But I've had the blessed assurance of the Presence of God saying,
    "Don't worry my child, I've got this."

# Suffer Well

When trials come upon you
That are out of your control
And you don't know where
To go or who to tell

Fall on your knees
Cry out to the Lord; Ask, "Please!"
For the strength to suffer well

When your sanity's in question
While learning life's lesson
But you feel as if you're
Literally going through hell
Cast all your cares
On the One who has bared all
Our sins on the Cross

When all of humanity was lost
Look to Jesus, and suffer well

When your body's racked with pain
There's only clouds and much rain
And the stormy seas of life began to swell
Place all that seems lost
At the foot of the Cross
Be thankful for Jesus sake
And suffer well

# Growing In My Knowledge Of God

"A tree will always be known by its fruit, and a true Christian will always be discovered by their habits, tastes, and affections."- J.C.Ryle

I am blessed to be in a Christ-centered church that teaches the word of God which is key to living an addiction-free life. And not just attending church, but getting involved in different ministries, attending a weekly Bible study, and getting into a Sheparding Group. If your church doesn't have small groups for accountability and encouragement of one another, this is a great opportunity to start one!

Surround yourself with godly people who aren't afraid to speak God's truth to you in love, and be open to receive that truth. Be sure that God is first on your mind first thing in the morning, throughout the day, and the last thing on your mind when you go to sleep at night. It certainly takes discipline, but practice makes perfect!

I believe a grateful heart - even when you don't feel like being grateful - is key in having a relationship with The Lord. Spend time with Him, not only in the morning, but before bed at night (again, it takes discipline!), thanking Him for another day, for getting through another day, and telling Him about your day. He's intently listening. I have several godly people in my life who have taught me how to pray God's word back to Him, and how to read God's word with The Holy Spirit's guidance. And please, don't be afraid or ashamed to ask for prayer, that is what the body of Christ is there for. They cannot bear your burdens if they don't know what they are. Do not allow the world, your flesh, and the devil to tell you that your burdens are no one's business, because then you're slipping into the abomination of pride and before long you will (and I'm speaking from experience) began to have the strut of a spiritual prig.

*"Bear one another's burdens and so fulfill the law of Christ."*
Galatians 6:2 ESV

# The Great High Priest

Jesus knows
    And understands
        Just how we feel
Which is why He came to live in a fallen world
    To be crucified, that we may be healed of
    The disease of sin
    Which rots us
    Body and soul
    Makes us enemies of God


Just to imagine our Lord in a manger
    Is a strange and wonderfully odd picture
    Of unconditional, unfailing love
    That we might become the righteousness of
                God
In Him,
The Risen Savior
    Who rightfully deserves our love and respect
Is The Great High Priest forever
    By the Order of Melchizedek.

So get your house in order

## Proclaim Christ Unashamedly Loud!

For soon and very soon,
    behold He comes
        Riding on the clouds!

# Six Hours One Friday

Six hours one Friday, the disciples wept
As they witnessed our Savior die a horrific death

When one of the thieves being crucified beside
mocked Jesus and spat out in a huff,
"If You are the Son of God
    Save Yourself
        And save us!"

The thief on the other side of Jesus
    Rebuked him
Surely, some who witnessed this rebuke thought it odd
when he says to him,
    "Hey, do you not fear God?
    You and I are criminals
    And our punishment is just
But this Man
    Has committed no crime and
        He's dying
            For us."

Hallelujah
    Our Savior,
        Oh no, did not stay dead!

He is Risen with all power, and of the church,
    He is the Head

When we are tempted to despair
    Complain
    And feel completely worn
Remember, Jesus didn't promise
    On this side of heaven
    A rose garden
    Without thorns.

After all
He wore a crown of them
On His precious brow for us.

# Revelation

I had always thought of Easter as being a time
Of brand-new clothes and shoes that shine
Never embracing the fact that
I Was a reason that Jesus came to die;

My sin-sick heart and blasphemous thoughts
Are what helped nail Him to that awful Cross

But the only thing that I was thinking at the time was,
    "Is this woman's dress
        More expensive than mine?"

Then one day as I sat reading in my room
All of a sudden I was filled with gloom at the
Conviction burning in my heart
Of Jesus shed blood

In tears of revelation
That it was in my place He stood.

    He is risen!
        Hallelujah!
            He is risen indeed!

# He Alone

I'm so glad this world is not
                      My home
That all my trust rests in Him
                      Alone

While still in this tent as I wail and lament
Soon my home shall be with The One who was sent

To bear the burden of my sin
That I may not have to enter in an eternity
        Apart from His holy face
          He daily gives me strength to run this race
                By His Spirit and amazing grace

For He alone is my Hope and Stay
        The Life
            The Truth
                And the ONLY Way!

    Hallelujah!
            He lives!

# Indescribable

Once upon a time, long ago
        Over 2000 years or so
In a tiny town called Bethlehem
          Was one born called The Great I AM

His birth, from centuries past, had been prophesied
When I heard that He was actually BORN boy, was I surprised

As I looked into the manger and said
        What?! What?! Are you crazy?
              This can't be Messiah
                    He's only a baby!

Later, three wise men from the East, they came
"Here is the King who's star we followed," they proclaimed.
As I looked in amazement at these three
The gifts that they brought with them gave me such clarity

The first gift was that of gold,
          A gift for a King
I thought in my heart,
      "Wow! What a glorious thing."

As the second gift was that of frankincense
From of its whiteness I thought,
    "Well sure
      If this Baby is God
      He would have to be pure."

Myrrh, the third gift I beheld
    As my eyes began to well up with a tear,
    As this last gift revealed the reason He was here:

        To die for all the sins of the world
        And reconcile us back to the Father as well
        And not have to spend an eternity in hell

Hallelujah!
    I cried after pondering this
    And praised God for His indescribable Gift!

Hallelujah Christ is born!

# A Poem for the Ladies

## I Know I'm Going to Heaven

I know I'm going to heaven some day

I'm gonna see my Savior one day

So get your house in order
      For He's coming back again

Ain't no two ways about it
      You're either out
      Or you're in

If you know Jesus, you can say of your soul
      "It is well."

If not let's face it, my friend
      You're on a road straight to hell.

So don't be a whitewashed tomb
And try and cover your sin with
      smooth talk,
      faithless work,
      fine clothes
      and paint

'Cause God knows
      In your heart
      If you're a saint or you ain't

# Phillipians 4:8

Whatsoever things
          Are true
Whatsoever things
          Are lovely
Whatsoever things
          Are of good report
    I want it more
    I want it more;

Whatsoever things
          Are excellent
Whatsoever things
          Are worthy of praise
Whatsoever things
          Are honest and true
    I want because they are all
    Reflections of You;

Every day He's the same
So give unto the Lord
The glory due His name

Your name is faithful and true
And we belong to You

And the God of peace will be
With your spirit
Always

# *An Invitation*

Lynn Irby is a "trophy of God's grace." Against all odds God reached down in divine grace and pulled Lynn "out of the miry clay and set her feet upon a rock." Lynn wants you to know that God is the God of the impossible. He took a life utterly dominated with the ravages of sin and transformed it by His redeeming grace into a life of praise and purpose. Lynn's story is a powerful testimony of God's amazing grace.

Would you like to know this amazing God? Jeremiah 33:3 says, "Call to me and I will answer you and show you great and mighty things which you cannot imagine." You might be saying "God wouldn't want me. I have nothing to offer. My life is a wreck." You are the very person God wants. Galatians 1:4 says, "Jesus gave Himself for our sins, that He might deliver us from this present evil world."

You see Jesus came to earth for one reason, to die for your sins. Romans 3:23 says, "All have sinned and come short of the glory of God." Romans 6:23 tells us that the wages of sin is death BUT the gift of God is eternal life through Jesus Christ our Lord." There is a hymn that says, "What can wash away my sin? Nothing but the blood of Jesus." He died and shed His blood to make a way for you to go to Heaven.

Romans 5:8 says, "But God proved His love toward us, in that, while we were yet sinners, Christ died for us." He died for you to make it possible for you to live with Him. John 3:16 says, "God so loved the world that He gave His only begotten Son that whosoever believeth in Him should not perish but have everlasting life."

Friend, you will die one day and when you die you will either live in Heaven or Hell for all of eternity. The only way anyone can go to Heaven is through Jesus Christ and His shed blood. You know you are a sinner. Confess your sins to Jesus. I John 1:9 says, "If you will confess your sins, He (Jesus) is faithful and will forgive your sins, and cleanse you from all unrighteousness."

Friend, would you right now ask Jesus to forgive your sins. Invite Him into your life. Ask Him to take control of your life and be your Savior and Lord. I John 5:11-13, "And this is the record that God hath given to us, eternal life, and this life is in His Son. He that hath the Son hath life; and he that hath not the Son of God hath not life. These things have I written unto you that believe on the name of the Son of God; that you may know that you have eternal life, and that you may believe on the name of the Son of God."

*Laura Baker*
*Founder*
*Prasso Ministries*

Made in the USA
Columbia, SC
27 June 2025